Contents

ACKNOWLEDGEMENTS

Illustrations

Cover: backdrop: Getty images / © H. Armstrong Roberts, car: Getty images / © Car Culture; **pp. 4, 7, 26, 27, 29, 30, 33, 34, 35, 36, 37, 38, 39, 40, 41, 42, 43, 44, 45, 46:** all stills taken from *The Great Gatsby*, 1974, a film by Jack Clayton, screenplay: Francis Ford Coppola (after F. Scott Fitzgerald), with Robert Redford, Mia Farrow et. al.), © Paramount Pictures, Los Angeles; **p. 8 top:** © Courtesy of the Library of Congress / © 2003 Jone Johnson Lewis (modifications) / original copyright: E. W. Gustin; **bottom:** © 1922, Harold Rossiter Music Company, Chicago; **p. 9 top:** Getty images / Hulton Archive, **bottom:** Getty images / Hulton Archive / General Photographic Agency; **p. 10 top:** Getty images / Hulton Archive / Seeberger Freres, **bottom:** Getty images / Hulton Archive; **p. 14:** © Francis Cugat / Charles Scribner's Sons, 1925, New York / Collectors Reprints, Inc., New York.

They're careless people, Tom and Daisy.
They smash things up and they retreat into their money, or vast carelessness, or whatever it is that keeps them together, leaving other people to clean up the mess.

Nick Carraway

Liebe Schülerinnen und Schüler,

in diesem Heft finden Sie Vorschläge zur Auseinandersetzung mit dem Film *The Great Gatsby*.

Der Verfasser des Romans *The Great Gatsby*, Scott Fitzgerald, gehört zu den Autoren, die das Lebensgefühl einer ganzen Generation prägten und thematisierten. Es ist das Lebensgefühl der *Lost Generation*, das in den 20er und 30er Jahren des letzten Jahrhunderts durch die Werke von Faulkner, Fitzgerald und Hemingway eine Ausdrucksform fand.

Fitzgeralds wohl bekanntester Roman *The Great Gatsby* personifiziert und ikonisiert diese Lebensphilosophie; eine cineastische Entsprechung wurde 1974 durch den gleichnamigen Film mit den Protagonisten Robert Redford und Mia Farrow geschaffen, der Thema dieses Arbeitsheftes ist.

Momentan erfährt Fitzgeralds Werk eine Renaissance – wohl nicht nur durch die Implementierung dieses Stoffes in die Vorgaben für das Zentralabitur. Vielleicht wäre gerade deshalb und auch zur besseren Vermittlung an die aktuelle Zuschauergeneration eine zeitgemäßere Inszenierung, wie zum Beispiel im Falle von Effi Briest, wünschenswert – obwohl Robert Redford und Mia Farrow als Ikonen der 70er und 80er Jahre Gatsby und Daisy beinahe idealtypisch verkörpern.

Die Bezeichnung des Protagonisten als *great* im Roman- wie auch im Filmtitel erinnert an große Persönlichkeiten der Geschichte, wie Alexander den Großen, Peter den Großen, Karl den Großen und viele andere. Es bleibt abzuwarten und gegebenenfalls zu diskutieren, ob und warum diese Qualifizierung für Gatsby angemessen ist.

Gatsby – soviel sei hier bereits verraten – ist jedenfalls eine schillernde Persönlichkeit, von der der Erzähler der Geschichte, Nick Carraway, gleich zu Beginn behauptet: ... [*he had*] *an extraordinary gift for hope, a romantic readiness such as I have never found in any other person and which is not likely I shall ever find again. No – Gatsby turned out right in the end.*

Gatsby selbst behauptet von sich, als dekorierter Kriegsheld mit Drogeriemärkten und einem großen Erbe seinen Reichtum erworben zu haben. Es kursieren aber auch andere Gerüchte über ihn: Er sei ein *bootlegger*, also ein Alkoholschmuggler, habe einen Menschen auf dem Gewissen usw. Diese Gerüchte entstehen vor allem deshalb, weil Gatsby eher zurückgezogen in seiner Villa lebt. Er organisiert zwar regelmäßig große Partys auf seinem Anwesen, nimmt an diesen selbst aber nicht teil, sondern lässt sich nur berichten, wer anwesend ist. Später erfährt der Zuschauer, dass er diese Partys nur veranstaltet, weil er hofft, dort seine Jugendliebe Daisy Fay wieder zu treffen, die in der Nachbarschaft lebt, aber inzwischen mit Tom Buchanan verheiratet ist.

Gleichzeitig thematisiert der Film – wie auch der Roman – das amerikanische Leben in den sogenannten *Roaring Twenties* und den *American Dream.* All diese Aspekte haben wir in unsere Arbeitsanregungen aufgenommen.

Dazu werden im ersten Teil des Heftes – *Information about the film* – zunächst Hintergrundinformationen zum Film gegeben, um eine zeitliche und inhaltliche Einordnung zu erleichtern.

Im zweiten Kapitel – *Let's watch the film* – steht der rein inhaltliche Aspekt des Filmes im Vordergrund, bevor wir uns im dritten Kapitel – *Let's analyse the film* – der eigentlichen Filmanalyse widmen. Dabei haben wir uns vor allem auf die unterschiedlichen Charaktere und deren Beziehung zueinander konzentriert, es werden aber auch die Handlungsorte genauer untersucht.

Im letzten Kapitel – *Evaluation* – geht es dann um die Bewertung des Films, unter anderem anhand einer *Review.*

Das Filmheft ist so angelegt, dass Sie sich den Film eigenständig erarbeiten können. Falls Ihnen eine Aufgabe Schwierigkeiten bereitet, schauen Sie nach unter www.cornelsen.de/abi-e (dort das Cover des Heftes anklicken). Die Anmerkungen, die Sie dort abrufen und für sich überprüfen können, sind nicht einfach als „richtige" Lösungen gedacht, sondern als Wegweiser für Ihre weitere Arbeit.

Unter derselben Adresse finden Sie zur Diskussion der filmischen Präsentation der Themen auch das ► Worksheet *Selected terms for film analysis* zum Nachschlagen der wichtigsten Film-Termini.

Gutes Gelingen wünschen Ihnen

Christiane Mayer

Henning Sonntag

The plot

The main characters come from the Middle West of the USA, but the action is situated in New York and Long Island, among the rich and wealthy. James Gatz from Dakota, whose childhood and road to success remains veiled and foggy throughout the story, realizes one day that social success correlates with the personal image. He therefore assumes the persona of the dynamic and handsome Jay Gatsby, who convincingly plays the role of the self-made successful man, although actual material success is still far from his grasp. By a stroke of good fortune a millionaire takes him on as private secretary and sails with him around the world.

As a young officer Gatsby falls in love with Daisy Fay, a rich girl from Louisville, Kentucky, but upon his being called up to go to war in 1917 she breaks off the relationship on the grounds that he lacks the money to get married. Instead Daisy marries a rich and insensitive sportsman from Chicago, Tom Buchanan. Tom, Daisy and their little three-year-old daughter live in East Egg on Long Island in the summer of 1922, when the film begins.

On the other side of the bay is West Egg, where Jay Gatsby has bought an impressive estate, in which he celebrates lavish parties. Every night Gatsby stands alone at the water's edge gazing at the green lantern which marks the Buchanans' estate. He dreams of turning back the last five years in order to win back Daisy's love.

Another central figure is Nick Carraway, the narrator of the story. Nicks portrays the events of 1924 after he had returned home to the Middle West. Nick is 30 years old and has just finished Yale University. He comes as a bond salesman to New York in 1922 to learn the bond business. He rents a modest cottage next to Gatsby's estate and is fascinated by the mysterious, dandified behaviour of his rich neighbour.

As the film progresses he gets to know Gatsby better and better. Gatsby presents a clichéd picture of his life as a wealthy dilettante and war hero and convinces Nick, among other things, by showing him his war medals. In New York Gatsby introduces a bemused Nick to the underworld figure Meyer Wolfshiem, who is said to be the father of Gatsby's success. With the help of Gatsby's subterfuge string-pulling Nick manages to arrange a meeting with his cousin Daisy, after which Gatsby and Daisy fall in love again.

Tom, who has been conducting a long love affair with Myrtle Wilson, the spirited wife of a poor gas station tenant, does not allow Daisy to have an affair. During a trip to town Gatsby, Daisy and Tom have a row over this, and the tragedy takes its course when, on their way home to West Egg, Daisy accidentally runs over Myrtle Wilson while at the wheel of Gatsby's car. Tragically, Myrtle had actually been trying to escape from her husband at that moment, after he had become aware of his wife's second life.

Daisy drives on after the accident without helping Myrtle. Tom and Nick, in the car following Gatsby and Daisy, discover the dead Myrtle, and Tom tells George Wilson – who doesn't know that Tom was Myrtle's lover – that it was Gatsby with whom Myrtle had been having an affair. Stunned by this development, Wilson takes a gun and kills Gatsby in his swimming pool, subsequently committing suicide himself.

Following this catastrophe, Tom and Daisy, who have restated their personal commitment to one another, leave West Egg in a hurry.

Nick has to look after Gatsby's estate. At Gatsby's funeral there is only one mourner: his father from Dakota.

Nick decides to leave New York, disillusioned by these events. He comes to the conclusion that people like the Buchanans are careless people. In the end Nick realizes that he is unable to live the life of the East; even the Great Gatsby, the legendary bootlegger and scalper who tried to turn back time with the help of his platonic love, was defeated in the face of the overwhelming materialism of the age.

Gatsby symbolizes one of Fitzgerald's major leitmotifs – the search for the second chance.

The Great Gatsby
(1974)

Directed by	Jack Clayton
Writing credits	Francis Ford Coppola
Produced by	David Merrick

Cast

Jay Gatsby	Robert Redford
Daisy Buchanan	Mia Farrow
Tom Buchanan	Bruce Dern
Myrtle Wilson	Karen Black
Nick Carraway	Sam Waterston
Jordan Baker	Lois Chiles
Meyer Wolfshiem	Howard Da Silva
Mr. Gatz	Roberts Blossom

Chapters

1 Opening credits
2 The East Egg
3 Myrtle Wilson
4 Invitation
5 Lunch with Gatsby
6 Reacquainted
7 Rich and poor
8 A party for Daisy
9 Lovers
10 Going to town
11 Confronting Tom
12 Trouble on the road
13 The driver
14 Revenge
15 Put to rest

Historical background of the film: America during the 'Roaring Twenties'

Demobilization:
Sending home soldiers at the end of a war

At the end of World War I, soldiers returned to the United States with money in their pockets, finding many new products on the market to spend it on.

Lost Generation

The *Lost Generation* were young people who came out of World War I disillusioned and cynical about the world. The term usually refers to American writers who lived in Paris at the time, e.g. Ernest Hemingway, F. Scott Fitzgerald and Gertrude Stein.

Suffrage

On August 18, 1920, the *Nineteenth Amendment* granting women the right to vote was ratified by the last state:

'The right of citizens of the United States to vote shall not be denied or abridged by the United States or by any State on account of sex. Congress shall have power to enforce this article by appropriate legislation.'

The changing role of women

With the ratification of the 19th Amendment women finally attained political equality. This led to a generational gap between the 'new' women of the 20s and the previous generation. Whereas the previous generation thought that women could either have a career or a family, the 'new' women began to desire both. Thus the 'new' woman was less involved in social service than the previous generations, and in tune with the capitalistic spirit of the era, she was eager to compete and to find personal fulfilment.

Moreover, supported by the publications of Sigmund Freud and others, young women began to take part in the sexual liberation of their generation. They held the view that sex was not only central to the human experience but that women were sexual beings with human impulses and desires just like men and that restraining these impulses was self-destructive.

Prohibition Bootlegging Speakeasy

The 18th Amendment of the American Constitution made the manufacture, sale, import and export of alcohol illegal. The so-called *Prohibition* was greatly supported by churches and was enacted to alleviate social problems. However, America's continued desire for alcohol led to the rise of organized crime, smuggling (bootlegging) and gangster organizations all over the US. One famous gangster was Chicago's Al Capone.

Establishments where people could buy alcohol were known as *speakeasies*, i.e. places where people had to whisper (*speak easy*) when they wanted to order alcohol, so that they would not be overheard by passers-by. To run a *speakeasy* was very lucrative and thus during the time of the *Prohibition* they became more and more popular, despite the owners' risk of being arrested.

- Project: Find out about the famous Al Capone and make a presentation about him in front of the class.

The Jazz Age

In 1922 the first commercial radio station began broadcasting in Pittsburgh. Subsequently other radio stations spread quickly and with them the popularity of jazz. The music became associated with all things modern, sophisticated, and also decadent.

Louis Armstrong marked the time with improvisations and endless variations on a single melody. Apart from the clarinet, Sidney Bechet popularized the saxophone. Dance venues increased the demand for professional musicians and jazz adopted the 4/4 beat of dance music. At the end of the *Roaring Twenties*, Duke Ellington initiated the big-band era.

Dance

Starting in the 1920^{s}, ballrooms across the US sponsored dance contests, where dancers invented, tried, and competed with each other in new moves. Electric lighting made evening social entertainment more comfortable, giving rise to an era of dance halls and live music. The most popular dances were the foxtrot, waltz, tango, Charleston, and Lindy Hop.

From the early 1920^{s}, a variety of eccentric dances were developed. The first of these were the breakaway and Charleston. Both were based on black music styles and beats, including the widely popular blues.

Fashion

Young women's fashion of the 1920s was both a trend and a social statement, a breaking-off from the rigid Victorian way of life. These young, rebellious, middle-class women, called *flappers* by older generations, did away with the corset and wore knee-length dresses which exposed their legs and arms instead. The hairstyle of the decade was a chin-length bob, of which there were several popular variations. Make-up, which until the 1920s was not typically accepted in American society because of its association with prostitutes, became for the first time extremely popular.

Immigration

The United States became much more xenophobic or, at least, anti-immigrant.

Theodore Lothrop Stoddard (1883–1950), an American political scientist, historian, journalist, anthropologist, eugenicist, pacifist, and anti-immigration advocate published a number of books in which he argued that race and heredity were the guiding factors of history and civilization, and that the elimination or absorption of the 'white' race by 'coloured' races would result in the destruction of Western civilization.

Cars

The first production Model T Ford was assembled at the Piquette Avenue Plant in Detroit on October 1, 1908. Over the next 19 years, Ford would build 15,000,000 automobiles with the Model T engine.

The 'American Dream'

The *American Dream* represents the national ethos of the United States of America with its democratic and religious ideals holding out the promise of prosperity for its people: Every citizen of every rank can achieve a better, richer and happier life by hard work and individual strength. One metaphor for this dream is the phrase 'from rags to riches', symbolizing the possible career path from dishwasher to millionaire. The slogan was originally coined during the economic boom in the first part of the 20th century and made thousands of people immigrate to the USA, the land of hope, the land of the free.

The idea of the the *American Dream* is also rooted in basic parts of the *Declaration of Independence*, which states that all men are created equal, that they are endowed by their Creator with certain inalienable rights and that among these are life, liberty and the pursuit of happiness. The *American Dream* has evolved throughout history, beginning with the availability of land and the expansion to the west of the continent, ending with the exploration of space. The last frontier has always been regarded as a challenge to the imagination as well as a concrete obstacle to be overcome.

Today the *American Dream* most often refers to the aim of bringing personal prosperity or, with reference to the phrase *Pax Americana*, of bringing peace to the whole world. The *American Dream* has also become a literary leitmotif, as reflected, for example, in works like *Of Mice and Men* by John Steinbeck, *Death of a Salesman* by Arthur Miller and, certainly, *The Great Gatsby* by Scott Fitzgerald.

But no one has ever expressed the idea of this dream better than Walt Whitman (1819–1892), one of the most influential American poets, in *For You, O Democracy* (1860).

For You, O Democracy

Come, I will make the continent indissoluble,
I will make the most splendid race the sun ever shone upon,
I will make divine magnetic lands,
With the love of comrades,
With the life-long love of comrades.

I will plant companionship thick as trees along all the rivers of America,
and along the shores of the great lakes, and all over the prairies,
I will make inseparable cities with their arms about each other's necks,
By the love of comrades,
By the manly love of comrades.

For you these from me, O Democracy, to serve you ma femme!
For you, for you I am trilling these songs.

Indissoluble firm and lasting • *divine* godlike • *trill* sound made by the voice or as in bird song • *ma femme* (French) my wife

The 'American Dream' in F. Scott Fitzgerald's novel 'The Great Gatsby'

Nick Carraway, a young Midwesterner, came to New York in order to make his fortune. At the beginning he was fascinated by the wealth and energetic spirit of the society he had entered. Especially for him the figure of Jay Gatsby symbolized *the American Dream*, an icon of material success, since he had started out in life as a poor man and ended up being extraordinarily rich: *from rags to riches.*

Having spoken to Wolfshiem Nick begins to see through Gatsby and realizes that Gatsby's way of life has been financed by bootlegging and other criminal activities. But he also realizes that people like Tom and Daisy Buchanan, representatives of the upper, leisured classes, were simply frivolous, unprincipled people, in a way even worse than Gatsby, who after all was just following a dream:

They were careless people, Tom and Daisy – they smashed up things and creatures and then retreated back into their money or their vast carelessness, or whatever it was that kept them together, and let other people clean up the mess they had made ...

F. Scott Fitzgerald: The Great Gatsby, *p. 156.*

With the protagonist Jay Gatsby Fitzgerald effectively embodies a romantic idealism that is sustained and destroyed by the intensity of his own dreams. Nick Carraway, the narrator, engages the reader in the depiction of Gatsby's flawed grandeur and in the characterizations of Gatsby's love, Daisy and her husband, Tom Buchanan, Tom's mistress, Myrtle Wilson, and her pallid husband, George. Expertly constructed and marvellously evocative of the inner emptiness of the *Jazz Age's* beautiful people (cf. p. 9), the novel has the air of myth.

Few readers can escape perceiving in it the conflict between materialism and idealism that created and still defines the American character.

Questions on the film

- Daisy and Tom Buchanan, Myrtle and George Wilson, Jordan Baker, Nick Carraway and Jay Gatsby – what kind of people are they?
  Write brief characterizations of each of them (perhaps in groups).
  Explain what you know about the characters' past and their family background, their living conditions, their interests/hobbies, their outward appearance and about what is important to them in their lives.

- Outline the relationships between men and women in *The Great Gatsby*.
  Are there any parallels between the couples?

- Would you call Gatsby a tragic figure? Discuss.

- Gatsby has apparently made it *from rags to riches*. Would you say that he could be called the personification of the *American Dream*? Discuss.

- Imagine you worked in a shop where the DVD is sold and you had to assign the film to a certain genre: Love, Political, Crime, Satire. Where would you put it and why?

- Nick Carraway warns Gatsby that he *cannot repeat the past* [1:14:18–1:15:47].
  Briefly explain in what context this statement is made and then discuss it.

- After Gatsby's funeral Nick meets Jordan in a restaurant [2:12:08–2:14:51].
  Nick complains that Daisy has not even sent a condolence message.
  Explain Jordan's reaction in the context of the film.

- When Nick Carraway asks Meyer Wolfshiem to come to Gatsby's funeral, Wolfshiem declines, saying that one should *learn to show* [one's] *friendship for a man when he is alive and not after he is dead.* [2:06:02–2:07:46]. Nick remembers that Wolfshiem said the same when he first met him in a bar and was talking about another friend who had been shot. Discuss Wolfhiem's point of view.

- How does the film illustrate the American lifestyle during the so-called *Roaring-Twenties*?

- Only after completing the novel did Fitzgerald make a final decision about the title of his novel. Other ideas of his were:

  Among Ash-Heaps and Millionaires
  Trimalchio in West Egg*
  On the Road to West Egg
  Under the Red, White and Blue
  Gold-Hatted Gatsby
  The High-Bouncing Lover

  Comment on these titles.

- Watch the film and explain how Gatsby's death is foreshadowed. Take into consideration both the dialogue and the pictures.

- Neither in the novel nor in the film is Gatsby's story told chronologically. What might the reason be for this decision?

- Discuss the meaning of the green light over a bay in front of the Buchanans' house.

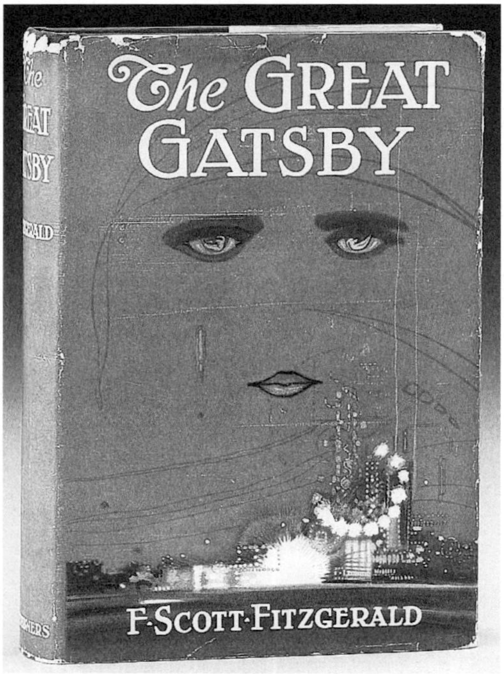

A little-known artist named Francis Cugat illustrated the book while Fitzgerald was still writing it. The cover was completed before the novel and Fitzgerald liked it so much that he told his publisher he had 'written it into' the novel.

- Describe the cover in detail and explain what Fitzgerald might have meant by saying he had 'written it into' the novel.

---

* *Trimalchio* is a former slave, released from slavery in the Roman novel *The Satyricon*. He has attained power and wealth through hard work and perseverance and is known for throwing lavish dinner parties where his numerous servants bring course after course of exotic delicacies.

Scene index

Chapter (Time)	Characters / Action
1	**Opening credits / The East Egg 0:00:00–0:13:43**
0:00:00–0:03:22	Opening credits / Introduction A tour through Gatsby's house: The viewers see his furniture, expensive decoration and photos of Daisy.
0:03:22–0:05:41	Nick Carraway is on his way from the West Egg to the East Egg by boat to visit his cousin Daisy. He is met by her husband Tom at the landing stage and accompanied to the house.
0:05:41–0:10:01	Tom leads Nick into the living-room, where he meets his cousin Daisy and Jordan Baker, a famous golf player. Later they decide to have a drink in the garden. During their conversation Jordan mentions Gatsby, which makes Daisy sit up. Moreover, Nick learns from Jordan that Tom 'has a woman in New York'. Daisy obviously knows that. Tom explains his theory about the submersion of the white race.
0:10:01–0:11:13	On his way back home Nick reflects on the afternoon and how his attitude will have changed by the autumn *(flash forward).* When he is back at his house, he sees Gatsby standing on the wall of his mansion looking over the bay.
0:11:13–0:13:44	The next day at his house Nick observes the events at his neighbour's: the preparation of the party and – in the evening – the party itself.
2	**Myrtle Wilson 0:13:44–0:26:40**
0:13:44–0:16:16	On their way to New York Tom and Nick stop at Wilson's garage in the Valley of Ashes. There Tom introduces 'his girl' (Myrtle Wilson) to Nick. Tom tells Myrtle to go to New York by train and to meet him there.
0:16:16–0:17:41	The men meet Myrtle at the station. On their way to their apartment Tom buys a dog for Myrtle from an old man.
0:17:41–0:23:25	A party at the apartment: Nick is introduced to Catherine, Myrtle's sister, who tells him what she has heard about Gatsby. Moreover, she explains that both Tom and Myrtle are very unhappy in their marriages. At the same time Myrtle recalls how she met Tom on a train. Although she really seems to be in love with Tom, the scene ends in a fight between the two, during which Tom hits Myrtle in the face.
0:23:25–0:23:58	Daisy is together with Tom during a reception at their house.
0:23:58–0:24:19	During sunset Nick can be seen looking over the bay.
0:24:19–0:26:40	While Jordan is playing golf, Nick and Daisy are sitting on a bench talking. Daisy informs Nick about her plans to arrange a marriage between Jordan and him. Moreover, she tells him about her unhappy marriage with Tom. When Tom joins them Daisy pretends to have talked about the submersion of the white race.
3	**Invitation 0:26:41–0:37:38**
0:26:41–0:26:48	Nick is invited to Gatsby's party.
0:26:49–0:30:01	The evening at Gatsby's party: Gatsby is walking around among the dancers. Then he meets Jordan, who wants to spend the evening with him. During a conversation between other party guests the viewers learn more rumours about Gatsby.
0:30:01–0:32:49	After scenes illustrating the decadence and affluence of society (drinking, dancing, fighting) a man tells Nick to follow him. Nick justifies himself and explains that he was invited to the party.

Chapter (Time)	Characters / Action
0:32:50–0:36:23	Nick is led into Gatsby's private rooms, where he finally meets him. Gatsby tells Nick that he wanted to make his acquaintance because they are neighbours. He suggests having lunch together the next day. During their conversation Gatsby receives a phone call. When leaving the room Nick seems puzzled, probably also because Gatsby mentioned that he did not like parties much, but invites a great number of people anyway.
0:36:23–0:37:38	Nick returns downstairs to join the party again .
4	**Lunch with Gatsby 0:37:39–0:43:16**
0:37:39–0:39:36	The next day Gatsby and Nick are looking at Gatsby's cars. On their way to a restaurant Gatsby tells Nick his version of his life story. He claims to be the son of rich parents, a decorated major in the war (World War I) and to have been educated at Oxford. Later he suggests that Nick joins his business, but when Nick wants to know what he does exactly he becomes evasive.
0:39:36–0:43:17	Nick is introduced to Meyer Wolfshiem and learns that he was very close to Rosy Rosenthal, a famous gangster, and that he is a gambler who 'fixed the 1919 World Series'. Before leaving the restaurant Nick meets Tom. The latter wonders how Nick can afford to eat at such a place.
5	**Reacquainted 0:43:17–0:57:03**
0:43:17–0:44:54	Jordan informs Nick that Gatsby wants him to invite Daisy for tea. By this he intends to arrange a meeting between the two of them.
0:44:54–0:45:56	Nick has agreed and meets Gatsby to talk about the details of the meeting.
0:45:56–0:46:20	Nick phones Daisy to invite her to his house.
0:46:21–0:46:50	Preparation of the meeting: Gatsby has Nick's house decorated for the occasion.
0:46:50–0:48:34	Gatsby himself comes over. Shortly before Daisy arrives he gets nervous and starts to doubt whether meeting her is a good idea.
0:48:35–0:51:04	Daisy arrives and enters Nick's house. While looking at the place, she suddenly notices Gatsby in the mirror. Nick introduces them but they admit that they know each other. Nick decides to leave them alone for a while.
0:51:04–0:53:21	Nick returns to his living-room and suggests having tea, but Gatsby wants to show Daisy around his house. While Nick and Gatsby are waiting outside for Daisy, Gatsby talks about his business again and starts contradicting himself.
0:53:21–0:57:04	Gatsby shows Daisy around his house. Daisy is deeply impressed. Later they have champagne. In his bedroom Gatsby shows Daisy all his shirts, takes them out of his wardrobe and throws them around. Daisy gets sentimental.
6	**Rich and Poor 0:57:04–1:06:32**
0:57:04–0:58:39	Various scenes: Jordan and Nick filling up the car at Wilson's garage, Tom and Myrtle together in a bedroom, Nick repairing his boat and looking over to Gatsby's house.
0:58:40–1:01:51	Gatsby and Daisy are together at Gatsby's house and talking about their past. Daisy learns that Gatsby has collected all newspaper articles about her in an album.
1:01:51–1:02:04	Daisy and Gatsby outside sitting on the lawn.
1:02:04–1:02:15	Myrtle is putting on make-up in front of a mirror. Tom can be seen in the background lying on a bed. Myrtle casts amorous glances at him.
1:02:15–1:06:32	Daisy is taken to Gatsby's by Jordan and runs over to his house. They continue their conversation and Gatsby reproaches Daisy for having married Tom and not having waited for him. Daisy tries to justify herself.

Chapter (Time)	Characters / Action
7	**A Party for Daisy 1:06:33–1:16:17**
1:06:33–1:14:18	One of Gatsby's parties: Tom arrives with Daisy and Jordan. At the party he recognizes many rich people. Later in the evening Daisy starts dancing with Gatsby. When Tom realizes this he gets annoyed and forces her to leave together with him. Daisy tries to provoke him by not listening, but then follows her husband.
1:14:18–1:15:47	Gatsby and Nick have a conversation after the party. Gatsby admits that he wants to win Daisy back, but Nick is convinced that one 'cannot repeat the past'.
1:15:47–1:16:18	During a fencing match Tom orders one of his servants to find out everything about Gatsby.
8	**Lovers 1:16:18–1:23:42**
1:16:18–1:17:21	Gatsby and Daisy are together in Gatsby's kitchen. Daisy asks Gatsby to put on his old uniform.
1:17:21–1:19:36	*Flashback:* Daisy and Gatsby are dancing together. Then they start kissing each other.
1:19:36–1:21:07	Gatsby gives Daisy a ring as a sign of his love to her. Daisy asks him to wear it for her because she cannot wear it. Then they kiss.
1:21:08–1:22:23	Tom's servant – allegedly a reporter from the *New York Journal* – asks Nick questions about Gatsby. Nick tells him to go directly to Gatsby.
1:22:23–1:22:35	Gatsby and Daisy are spending time together.
1:22:36–1:23:43	Nick is down at the sea, where he has found a dead bird. When he sees Gatsby on the wall at his house, he approaches him and wants to know if Gatsby intends to close his place down. Gatsby denies this and explains that he has fired his servants only to avoid gossip.
9	**Going to Town 1:23:43–1:34:34**
1:23:43–1:25:08	Gatsby and Daisy are together again. Gatsby wants Daisy to be honest and to tell her husband the truth. Daisy tells him to wait.
1:25:08–1:28:50	Daisy, Gatsby, Nick, Jordan and Tom are together at the Buchanans'. The atmosphere is very tense because Tom knows about the affair between Gatsby and his wife. Daisy suggests going to town and the others agree.
1:28:51–1:31:09	While the men are waiting outside the house for the women to get ready, Gatsby and Tom decide to swap cars. Daisy does not even try to hide her affection for Gatsby. She even refuses to get into the car with her husband, but tells him bluntly that she will go with Gatsby. Tom disapproves of her behaviour but does not contradict her.
1:31:10–1:34:34	Tom has to fill up his car and stops at Wilson's garage. Ironically, Wilson tells him that he is going to go west with his wife because he has learned that she is having an affair. Myrtle is locked in her room. In order to cry for help she breaks the window, but Tom does not notice her.
10	**Confronting Tom 1:34:35–1:41:31**
1:34:35–1:40:01	In New York they meet in a hotel room. Tom openly speaks about Daisy and Gatsby's affair, which causes an argument. Daisy announces that she is going to leave Tom, but Gatsby is not content because he wants her to add that she has never loved Tom. Tom insists that Daisy is never going to leave him and Daisy rushes out of the room.
1:40:01–1:40:34	Gatsby and Tom follow Daisy through the hotel restaurant. When Tom cannot reach her, he publicly announces that Gatsby is a 'bootlegger'.

Chapter (Time)	Characters / Action
1:40:35–1:41:31	Back in the hotel room, Tom offers Jordan and Nick a drink, but they decline. Nick mentions that it is his 30th birthday.
11	**Trouble on the Road 1:41:32–1:48:31**
1:41:32–1:43:36	Myrtle and her husband have a fight. Myrtle tries to escape. Her husband warns her that even if she thinks she can betray him, she cannot betray God.
1:43:37–1:46:08	Tom is on his way back from New York together with Jordan and Nick. At Wilson's garage they see many people. So they stop and find out that Myrtle was run over by 'a new yellow car' when she was trying to escape. George Wilson is very sad, while Tom seems to understand who was responsible for the accident.
1:46:08–1:47:22	Back at Tom's house, Nick refuses to come in. He wants to go home.
1:47:23–1:48:31	As he drives away, Nick sees Gatsby standing in front of the Buchanans' house. Gatsby asks Nick if Myrtle is dead. Then he tries to tell Nick that it was Daisy driving the car. Gatsby decides to wait in front of the house to protect Daisy from her husband.
12	**The Driver 1:48:32–1:56:18**
1:48:32–1:48:48	The damaged car can be seen.
1:48:48–1:52:26	A friend of Mr Wilson's tries to console him. Wilson is convinced that his wife was not killed in an accident, but deliberately run over by her lover because she recognized the car and ran towards it. However, the driver did not stop. Then Wilson shows his friend a valuable dog leash that he has found among Myrtle's things although they do not have a dog.
1:52:26–1:53:12	Wilson gets a paper bag ready and prepares to go and 'fix it'.
1:53:13–1:53:34	The damaged yellow car is driven out of Gatsby's garage.
1:53:35–1:56:18	Gatsby visits Nick at his house. He informs him that Daisy had been driving the car the night before.
13	**Revenge 1:56:19–2:07:46**
1:56:19–1:56:25	The green lights on the landing stage at the Buchanans' can be seen.
1:56:26–1:56:38	Tom and Daisy are sitting at the table. It seems that they have become reconciled and they gently touch each other.
1:56:39–1:58:28	Gatsby is thinking about Daisy and their love. Nick advises him to go away for a while, but Gatsby rejects that.
1:58:29–1:58:47	Wilson can be seen walking firmly along the road.
1:58:48–1:58:58	Gatsby is looking over the bay.
1:58:59–2:00:54	Wilson enters the Buchanans' ground and has a look at the garage. Suddenly he appears in front of their dining-room window. Tom talks to him alone, but when Daisy learns that this is the man from the garage she nearly has to throw up. However, her daughter distracts her. Mr Wilson shows Tom the dog leash, their words however cannot be heard.
2:00:55–2:02:11	Gatsby and Nick are at Gatsby's house. They talk about the passing summer and decide to meet at the pool later.
2:02:12–2:06:01	Gatsby goes to the pool, puts on a record and then relaxes on a lilo in the water. However, he is constantly distracted and calls Daisy's name. Wilson enters, takes out his gun, shoots Gatsby, then commits suicide.

Chapter (Time)	Characters / Action
2:06:02–2:07:46	Nick comments on the events. He is very disappointed because now that Gatsby is dead, nobody seems to be interested in him any more. Wolfshiem even refuses to attend Gatsby's funeral and Daisy has gone away with Tom. Still he hopes that she will phone or visit him.
14	**Put to Rest 2:07:47–2:17:31**
2:07:47–2:10:10	Instead of Daisy Gatsby's father arrives. He tells Nick how Gatsby broke up with him. It becomes clear that Gatsby's stories about his family were all made up.
2:10:11–2:11:39	Nick and Mr Gatsby, whose real name is Gatz, are on their way to the funeral. They drive past Wilson's garage and Nick sees Catherine tidying up there. Mr Gatz starts reading from one of Gatsby's books.
2:11:39–2:12:07	The funeral: Only the priest, Mr Gatz and Nick are present.
2:12:08–2:14:51	Nick is in a restaurant with Jordan. He complains about Tom and Daisy being superficial people since they have sent neither a message nor flowers to the funeral. Jordan does not seem to understand. When Tom appears he is surprised by Nick being completely reserved. He insists that he, too, suffered and that he just told Wilson – what he thought was – the truth about his wife's death. Just as Nick is about to tell Tom that it was Daisy who had been driving the car that killed Myrtle, Daisy enters. They leave, not seeming to realize what they have done.
2:14:51–2:15:15	Nick's final thoughts about Gatsby's dream to win Daisy back.

Viewing comprehension

- 1 What are the most striking things in Gatsby's house?
- 2 What are Nick Carraway's impressions on his way to the Buchanans?
- 3 What does Jordan Baker tell Nick about Tom's phone call?
- 4 Nick is on his way back home and reflects about the afternoon and the future. What filmic device is used to show this?
- 5 What does Nick observe the next day?
- 6 Where do Tom and Nick stop on their way to New York?
- 7 What does Myrtle's sister tell Nick about Gatsby?
- 8 What do Daisy and Nick talk about while Jordan is playing golf?
- 9 What kind of invitation does Nick receive?
- 10 What kind of rumours are spread about Gatsby at the party?
- 11 What do the film makers want to illustrate with the various scenes at Gatsby's party?
- 12 What is the result of Nick's talk to Gatsby and why is he puzzled in the end?
- 13 What does Gatsby tell Nick about his life on their way to the restaurant?
- 14 Who is Nick introduced to there?
- 15 What is Nick going to arrange in his cottage?
- 16 What happens when Daisy and Gatsby meet?
- 17 Why does Daisy get sentimental in Gatsby's house?
- 18 What do Daisy and Gatsby talk about when they meet again?
- 19 How does Daisy try to justify her reaction?
- 20 What happens at Gatsby's party when Tom, Daisy and Jordan are invited?
- 21 Why is Tom so annoyed in the end?
- 22 Why is Nick sceptical about Gatsby's wish to win Daisy back?

- **23** What does Tom order during a fencing match?
- **24** Why does Daisy ask Gatsby to put on his old uniform?
- **25** How does the rendezvous continue?
- **26** Why did Gatsby fire all his servants?
- **27** What happens when Daisy, Gatsby, Nick, Jordan and Tom are together at the Buchanans' house?
- **28** Why do they swap cars?
- **29** What does Tom learn when he stops at Wilson's garage to fill up?
- **30** What happens in the hotel room?
- **31** What is the reaction to Tom's accusation that Gatsby is a bootlegger?
- **32** Why does Nick mention his 30th birthday?
- **33** What happens at the Wilsons' garage? Why does Myrtle try to escape?
- **34** What do Tom and Nick find out on their way back home?
- **35** Why is Gatsby waiting in front of the Buchanans' house?
- **36** Why is George Wilson convinced that his wife was not killed in an accident?
- **37** What does Gatsby tell Nick about the accident?
- **38** What's the atmosphere like when Tom and Daisy are having lunch?
- **39** What happens when Daisy discovers George Wilson in front of the dining room?
- **40** What happens when Wilson enters Gatsby's house?
- **41** How does Nick comment on Wolfshiem's refusal to attend the funeral? What does he think of Daisy's behaviour?
- **42** What does Gatsby's father tell Nick?
- **43** What does Nick complain about when he is together with Jordan at the restaurant?
- **44** What is Tom's excuse when Nick accuses him of having told Wilson a lie?
- **45** How does Nick think about Gatsby at the end when he reflects on Gatsby's dream?

Map of New York and Long Island

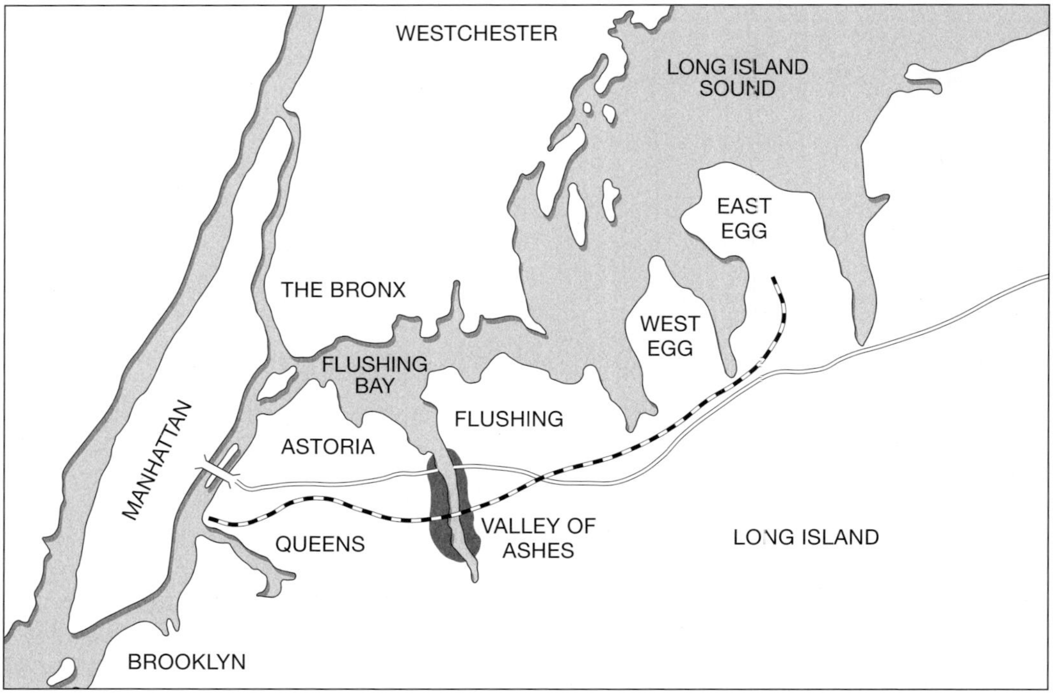

■ Assign the characters and the events to the places.

***Characters*:**
Daisy Buchanan • Tom Buchanan • Gatsby • Nick Carraway • Myrtle Wilson • George Wilson • Dr T. J. Eckleburg

***Events*:**
- Gatsby and Daisy admit that they are having an affair.
- Myrtle is killed in a car accident.
- Nick and Gatsby get to know Myrtle's sister Catherine.
- Gatsby is shot.
- Daisy meets her cousin Nick for the first time after the war again.
- Daisy meets Gatsby again.
- Tom meets Myrtle.
- Gatsby's parties.

The settings

New York and Long Island

Right at the beginning of the film/the novel we learn that Nick Carraway, Jay Gatsby and also Tom Buchanan have come to Long Island (East) from the Midwest, from Chicago.
In F. Scott Fitzgerald's novel the Midwest is described by Nick as *a country of wide lawns and friendly trees* (p. 7, l. 6).* Later, after Gatsby's death, he compares the East and the West.

Coming back west

One of my most vivid memories is of coming back west from prep school and later from college at Christmas time. Those who went farther than Chicago would gather in the old dim Union Station at six o'clock of a December evening with a few Chicago friends already caught up into their own holiday gayeties to bid them a hasty goodbye. I remember the fur coats of the girls returning from Miss This or That's and the chatter of frozen breath and the hands waving overhead as we caught sight of old acquaintances and the matchings of invitations: 'Are you going to the Ordways'? the Herseys'? the Schultzes'?' and the long green tickets clasped tight in our gloved hands. And last the murky yellow cars of the Chicago, Milwaukee & St. Paul Railroad looking cheerful as Christmas itself on the tracks beside the gate.

When we pulled out into the winter night and the real snow, our snow, began to stretch out beside us and twinkle against the windows, and the dim lights of small Wisconsin stations moved by, a sharp wild brace came suddenly into the air. We drew in deep breaths of it as we walked back from dinner through the cold vestibules, unutterably aware of our identity with this country for one strange hour before we melted indistinguishably into it again.

That's my middle-west – not the wheat or the prairies or the lost Swede towns but the thrilling, returning trains of my youth and the street lamps and sleigh bells in the frosty dark and the shadows of holly wreaths thrown by lighted windows on the snow. I am part of that, a little solemn with the feel of those long winters, a little complacent from growing up in the Carraway house in a city where dwellings are still called through decades by a family's name. I see now that this has been a story of the West, after all – Tom and Gatsby, Daisy and Jordan and I, were all Westerners, and perhaps we possessed some deficiency in common which made us subtly unadaptable to Eastern life.

1 *prep school = preparatory school* (in the USA) private secondary school preparing students for college
5 *gayeties* festivities
5 *bid sb. sth.* say sth. (e.g. a greeting or goodbye) to sb.
6 *Miss This or That's* many private girls' schools have names that begin with 'Miss'
6 *chatter* continuous rapid talk
8 *matching (n)* (here) comparison
10 *clasp sb./sth.* hold sb./sth. tightly
10 *murky* dark, dirty
15 *brace* (here) feeling or smell of freshness
17 *unutterable* cannot be said or put into words
22 *sleigh* Pferdeschlitten
22 *holly wreath* Kranz aus Stechpalmenzweigen
24 *complacent* generally satisfied with oneself
29 *subtle* not easy to detect or describe
29 *unadaptable* anpassungsunfähig

---

* Quotations from the novel are all taken from the *Cornelsen Senior English Library* edition of:
F. Scott Fitzgerald, *The Great Gatsby*, Berlin 2006.

Even when the East excited me most, even when I was most keenly aware of its superiority to the bored, sprawling, swollen towns beyond the Ohio, with their interminable inquisitions which spared only the children and the very old – even then it had always for me a quality of distortion. West Egg especially still figures in my more fantastic dreams. I see it as a night scene by El Greco: a hundred houses, at once conventional and grotesque, crouching under a sullen, overhanging sky and a lustreless moon. In the foreground four solemn men in dress suits are walking along the sidewalk with a stretcher on which lies a drunken woman in a white evening dress. Her hand, which dangles over the side, sparkles cold with jewels. Gravely the men turn in at a house – the wrong house. But no one knows the woman's name, and no one cares.

After Gatsby's death the East was haunted for me like that, distorted beyond my eyes' power of correction. So when the blue smoke of brittle leaves was in the air and the wind blew the wet laundry stiff on the line I decided to come back home.

The Great Gatsby, *pp. 152–154*

31 *sprawl* spread out loosely and irregularly over much space
31 *swell – swelled – swollen* become larger
31 *Ohio = Ohio River* river in the eastern USA
32 *inquisition (fml)* questioning about one's private affairs
35 *El Greco = Domenikos Theotocopoulos (1541–1614)* Spanish painter of Greek origin
36 *lustreless* without brightness or shine
38 *stretcher* covered frame on which a sick person can be carried by two people

The Midwest

The East

■ **1** Read the extract from the novel and write into the map values, attitudes and lifestyles that Nick associates with the East and the Midwest.

■ **2** Find out more information about the East and the Midwest and add this to your list.
http://en.wikipedia.org/wiki/Northeastern_United_States
http://en.wikipedia.org/wiki/Midwestern_United_States

The East and the West of the USA, East Egg and West Egg are contrasted by Nick Carraby:

I lived at West Egg, the, well, less fashionable of the two, though this is a most superficial tag to express the bizarre and not a little sinister contrast between them.

p. 8, ll. 26ff.

■ **3** Look at the map (p. 22) again and check who lives at East Egg and who lives at West Egg. Can the values and attitudes associated with the Midwest and the East of the United States also be ascribed to the characters? Explain why (not).

The Valley of Ashes

■ **4** Watch [0:11:13–0:16:16] and explain how the viewer, who has – together with Nick Carraway – just been an observer of one of Gatsby's parties is led to the Valley of Ashes.
Explain the effect that this has on the viewer.

■ **5** Describe the two settings – with help from the words in the box.
Check the meaning of the words and assign them to the different settings.
Be careful – some words and expressions might fit in both cases, others in none.
Explain your decisions.

affluence • close to the railway line • new lifestyle • decadence • lifelessness • death • immorality • desolation • greyish • prosperity • slapdashness • decency • colourful • destruction • music • American Dream • deceit • dinner parties • superficiality • ostentation • poverty • simplicity • sophistication • despair • hope • wealth • flappers • amusement • jealousy • pretense • upper class • lower class • degeneration • decay

Long Island	The Valley of Ashes

Nick tells the viewer that '*about half way between the two Eggs and New York the motor-road hastily joins the railroad and runs beside it for a short distance …*' [0:13:44–0:14:03].
So the inhabitants of the two Eggs have to drive through the so-called Valley of Ashes.

■ **6** What does this mean for the two worlds that are contrasted in this sequence?

Jay Gatsby –
How is the character introduced?

★ *You must go your way and I must go mine …
What'll I do when you are far away … what'll I do?
What'll I do with just a photograph to tell my troubles to?*

[0:00:00–0:03:22] Song text

★ *Gatsby? What Gatsby?*

[0:06:46–0:06:58] Daisy, after Jordan has mentioned Gatsby's name.

★ *At least once a fortnight a corps of caterers came down … with enough coloured lights to make a Christmas tree out of Gatsby's enormous gardens.*

[0:11:13–0:13:44] Nick Carraway

★ *By the autumn I would want no more privileged glimpses into the human heart. Only my neighbour Gatsby would be exempt from my reaction. Gatsby who represented everything for which I had an unaffected scorn. For Gatsby turned out alright in the end.
It was what preyed on him …*

[0:10:03–0:11:13] Nick Carraway

★ *There was music from my neighbour's house through those summer nights.
In his enchanted gardens men and girls came and went like moths among the whispering and champagne and the stars. They conducted themselves according to the rules of behaviour associated with an amusement park.*

[0:11:13–0:13:44] Nick Carraway

★ *I was just down on a party in West Egg … at a man called Gatsby …. He's German. Really. The cousin or nephew or something of Kaiser Wilhelm. That's where all his money comes from. … I'm scared of him.*

[0:18:30–0:19:38] Catherine at a party in New York

★ *When I was here last, I tore my gown on a chair and he asked my name.*
★ *Who's he?*
★ *Gatsby, of course.*
★ *Inside of a week, I got a package from Croirier's with a new evening gown! … It was gas blue with lavender beads, $265.*
★ *There's something funny about a fellow who does a thing like that.*
★ *He doesn't want any trouble with anyone.*
★ *Who?*
★ *Gatsby.*

[0:28:48–0:30:03] During a party at Gatsby's

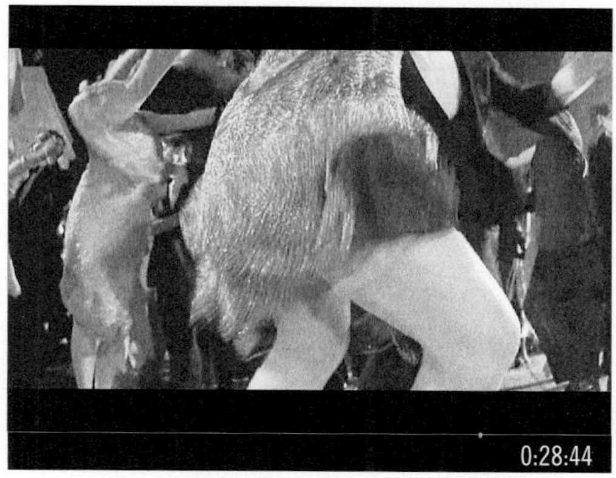

★ *Somebody told me they thought he'd killed a man once.*
★ *Killed a man? I heard he was connected with the government during the war, a spy.*
★ *I heard he was in oil, from a man who grew up with him in Texas.*
★ *I knew somebody who grew up with him in St Paul.*
★ *Look at him sometime, when he doesn't know anyone is looking. You can see it in his eyes. I bet he did kill a man.*
★ *Which one is he?*
★ *He never really goes to his own parties. Just looks to see who is here, then disappears.*

[0:28:48–0:30:03] During a party at Gatsby's

★ *How do you do, old sport, I'm Gatsby! …*
★ *I'm afraid, I'm not a very good host. …*
★ *Truth of the matter is: I don't much like parties!*
★ *I thought we should get acquainted since we are neighbours. …*
★ *I just thought perhaps we should meet. …*
★ *Perhaps we can have lunch some time? Tomorrow?*

[0:32:50–0:36:23] During a party at Gatsby's

Although the film/novel is called *The Great Gatsby* apart from one short moment [0:10:11–0:11:13], during which he is seen in front of his house, Gatsby appears only after 32 minutes.

Watch the film from [0:00:00–0:37:38].

■ **1** Look at the stills and the extracts from the dialogue. What impression do you get of Gatsby? Explain how this impression is achieved with the help of dialogue and filmic devices.
▸ Check *Selected terms for film analysis* for further information on film technique: www.cornelsen.de/abi-e

■ **2** Look at [0:10:45]: This is the first time we see Gatsby in the film.
Describe the camera range and camera angle in this still.
Say to what extent they help to create the viewers' impression of Gatsby.

Watch sequences [0:00:00–0:03:22] and [0:11:25–0:13:44] for a detailed analysis.

■ **3** Why does Gatsby really want to have lunch with Nick Carraway? What do you think?

Who is The Great Gatsby?

[0:37:39–0:43:17]

Gatsby: Look here, what's your opinion about me, anyhow?

Nick: I hadn't really thought about that.

Gatsby: Let me tell you something about my life. I don't want you to get the wrong impression from the stories you hear. I'm the son of wealthy people from the Midwest, all dead now. I was raised in America but educated at Oxford. It's a family tradition.
My family died and I came into a great deal of money. Then I lived in many capitals in Europe, trying to forget something sad that happened long ago. And then came the war. I was promoted to Major after I distinguished myself in battle. Every allied government gave me a decoration. ...

Nick: Why are you telling me this?

Gatsby: You don't make much money, do you? You sell bonds?
You see, I run a small business on the side. And I thought you might want to pick up an extra bit of money.

Nick: What kind of business exactly?

Gatsby: I'd like you to meet a friend of mine.

Gatsby with Nick on his way to a restaurant

Meyer Wolfshiem:	Gatsby?!
	Gatsby leaves
	He's a fine fellow, isn't he? Handsome to look at and a perfect gentleman. He was educated at Oxford College.
Nick:	Have you known Gatsby for a long time?
Meyer Wolfshiem:	Known him? I made him! I had the pleasure to make his acquaintance just after the war. He was so poor, he wore his uniform, 'cause he couldn't buy clothes.

Gatsby:	Look, my house shows up well, doesn't it? It took me just three years to earn the money that bought it.
Nick:	I thought you said you inherited your money?
Gatsby:	I did, old sport, but I lost most of it in the big panic. In the panic of the war.
Nick:	What business are you really in?
Gatsby:	That's my affair. ... I'm sorry. I've been in several things. The drugstore business, then oil. But I'm not in either one now.

■ **1** Read the extracts from the film dialogue and write down the thoughts and feelings Nick might have during his conversation with Gatsby.

What's your opinion of me, anyhow?

And then came that disconcerting ride. We hadn't reached West Egg Village before Gatsby began leaving his elegant sentences unfinished and slapping himself indecisively on the knee of his caramel-colored suit.

'Look here, old sport,' he broke out surprisingly. 'What's your opinion of me anyhow?'

A little overwhelmed I began the generalized evasions which that question deserves.

'Well, I'm going to tell you something about my life,' he interrupted. 'I don't want you to get a wrong idea of me from all these stories you hear.'

So he was aware of the bizarre accusations that flavored conversation in his halls.

'I'll tell you God's truth.' His right hand suddenly ordered divine retribution to stand by. 'I am the son of some wealthy people in the middle-west – all dead now. I was brought up in America but educated at Oxford because all my ancestors have been educated there for many years. It is a family tradition.'

He looked at me sideways – and I knew why Jordan Baker had believed he was lying. He hurried the phrase 'educated at Oxford,' or swallowed it or choked on it as though it had bothered him before. And with this doubt his whole statement fell to pieces and I wondered if there wasn't something a little sinister about him after all.

'What part of the middle-west?' I inquired casually.

'San Francisco.'

'I see.'

'My family all died and I came into a good deal of money.'

His voice was solemn as if the memory of that sudden extinction of a clan still haunted him. For a moment I suspected that he was pulling my leg but a glance at him convinced me otherwise.

'After that I lived like a young rajah in all the capitals of Europe – Paris, Venice, Rome – collecting jewels, chiefly rubies, hunting big game, painting a little, things for myself only, and trying to forget something very sad that had happened to me long ago.'

With an effort I managed to restrain my incredulous laughter. The very phrases were worn so threadbare that they evoked no image except that of a turbaned 'character' leaking sawdust at every pore as he pursued a tiger through the Bois de Boulogne.

'Then came the war, old sport. It was a great relief and I tried very hard to die but I seemed to bear an enchanted life. I accepted a commission as first lieutenant when it began. In the Argonne Forest I took two machine-gun detachments so far forward that there was a half mile gap on either side of us where the infantry couldn't advance. We stayed there two days and two nights, a hundred and thirty men with sixteen Lewis guns, and when the infantry came up at last they found the insignia of three

1 *disconcerting* causing sb. to feel embarrassed
14 *retribution (fml)* punishment given for causing injury, etc.
24 *San Francisco* city in the Far West (not in the Mid-West)
28 *pull sb.'s leg (infml)* make fun of sb.
30 *rajah* Indian king or prince
31 *big game* wild animals, e.g. lions, hunted for sport
35 *threadbare* too often used or too well known to be effective
36 *turbaned* wearing a turban
37 *Bois de Boulogne* park in Paris
40 *Argonne Forest* battle in eastern France between the Aisne and Meuse rivers in late 1918
41 *detachment* group of soldiers with a special task

German divisions among the piles of dead. I was promoted to be a major and every Allied government gave me a decoration – even Montenegro, little Montenegro down on the Adriatic Sea!'

Little Montenegro! He lifted up the words and nodded at them – with his smile. The smile comprehended Montenegro's troubled history and sympathized with the brave struggles of the Montenegrin people. It appreciated fully the chain of national circumstances which had elicited this tribute from Montenegro's warm little heart. My incredulity was submerged in fascination now; it was like skimming hastily through a dozen magazines.

He reached in his pocket and a piece of metal, slung on a ribbon, fell into my palm.

'That's the one from Montenegro.'

To my astonishment the thing had an authentic look. Orderi di Danilo, ran the circular legend, Montenegro, Nicolas Rex.

'Turn it.'

Major Jay Gatsby, I read, For Valour Extraordinary.

'Here's another thing I always carry. A souvenir of Oxford days. It was taken in Trinity Quad – the man on my left is now the Earl of Doncaster.'

It was a photograph of half a dozen young men in blazers loafing in an archway through which were visible a host of spires. There was Gatsby, looking a little, not much, younger – with a cricket bat in his hand.

Then it was all true. I saw the skins of tigers flaming in his palace on the Grand Canal; I saw him opening a chest of rubies to ease, with their crimson-lighted depths, the gnawings of his broken heart.

'I'm going to make a big request of you today,' he said, pocketing his souvenirs with satisfaction, 'so I thought you ought to know something about me. I didn't want you to think I was just some nobody. You see I usually find myself among strangers because I drift here and there trying to forget the sad thing that happened to me.' He hesitated. 'You'll hear about it this afternoon.'

'At lunch?'

'No, this afternoon. I happened to find out that you're taking Miss Baker to tea.'

'Do you mean you're in love with Miss Baker?'

'No, old sport, I'm not. But Miss Baker has kindly consented to speak to you about this matter.'

I hadn't the faintest idea what 'this matter' was, but I was more annoyed than interested. I hadn't asked Jordan to tea in order to discuss Mr. Jay Gatsby. I was sure the request would be something utterly fantastic and for a moment I was sorry I'd ever set foot upon his overpopulated lawn.

The Great Gatsby, *pp. 59–62*

51 *elicit sth. (from sb.) (fml)* draw sth. (e.g. information) from sb., usu. with difficulty
52 *incredulity* feeling of disbelief
53 *skim through sth.* glance through sth. (e.g. a book) without reading word for word
61 *valour (fml)* bravery (esp. in war)
63 *Trinity Quad* the quadrangle or courtyard of Trinity College, Oxford University
64 *loaf (v) (infml)* spend time idly
65 *host* large number
65 *spire* Turmspitze
68 *Grand Canal* the main waterway in Venice
69 *gnawing* continual distress and pain

■ **2** Read the extract from the novel and compare your ideas with the thoughts and feelings the narrator Nick reveals to the reader in the novel.

■ **3** If you had to film the extract from the novel, how would you make Nick's feelings clear to the viewer? In groups develop a film script and present your ideas to the class.
▸ Check *Selected terms for film analysis* for further information on film technique: www.cornelsen.de/abi-e

Time	**Dialogue**	**Characters** Who can be seen? What are they doing? Facial expressions Body language	**Camera** What do you want to show? – details shown by camera – camera angle – camera range – camera movement	**Sound**	**Other comments**
0:00:00					

■ **4** Compare your film script with the film. How does the director try to make Nick's thoughts clear to the viewer?

The truth about Gatsby?

Watch [2:07:47–2:12:07].

■ **5** Summarize what you learn about Gatsby's past from his father.

■ **6** Gatsby has obviously broken up with his dad, Mr Gatz. Comment on what his father thinks about this.

Watch the sequence again.

■ **7** Explain what filmic devices are used to underline the sadness in this sequence.

■ **8** Imagine Nick Carraway made a speech at Gatsby's grave. What would he have said about him? Write his speech.

Tom and Daisy Buchanan

★ *They're careless people, Tom and Daisy. They smash things up and they retreat into their money, or vast carelessness, or whatever it is that keeps them together, leaving other people to clean up the mess.*

[2:12:22] Nick Carraway

The whole plot of the film is about the development of Daisy Buchanan's and Jay Gatsby's relationship. In their younger years they had been a couple. They separated when Gatsby served in the army. Coming back home from war, Gatsby was confronted with Daisy's new decision: She had married the rich Tom Buchanan.

1:02:19

1:00:01

■ **1** Evaluate these stills and explain Daisy Buchanan's renewed fascination for Jay Gatsby.

1:01:31

Myrtle Wilson from the Valley of Ashes is fascinated by Tom Buchanan.

■ **2** Why does Myrtle feel attracted to Tom? Compare Daisy's and Myrtle's relationships with Tom.

■ **3** Compare the lives and the impressive houses of the two protagonists: Tom Buchanan and Jay Gatsby. What is the most striking difference in the wealth of the two?

Tom, Daisy and Gatsby come together for a decisive moment in their lives when they go together to the Plaza Hotel, where Gatsby forces a showdown with his remark:

■ **4** Describe Daisy's reaction when replying to Gatsby's request.

■ **5** What filmic devices are used to show Daisy's extraordinary emotional suspense?

Gatsby's romantic idealism has been crushed within a few seconds. He had always believed in Daisy's love and now has to realize that Daisy is prepared to sacrifice his love on the altar of wealth and exclusive position.

■ **6** Who is the winner in this sequence? How does the film present him?

Daisy's flirtation is over and moments later the sequence in the dining room shows Tom and Daisy's reunion.

■ **7** Analyse the stills and explain by what filmic means the process of reunion is visualized.

■ **8** Bearing in mind the sequence with Tom and Daisy sitting at the table in the Buchanans' dining room, look at the reasons why Daisy and Gatsby had to break up again.

■ **9** In what way do the stills give evidence of Tom and Daisy's 'carelessness'?

Further studies:

■ **10** Give evidence from the film that Fitzgerald has succeeded in vividly portraying the other side of The *American Dream* – the economic, social, even moral decay. Give a description of social life at the time, as presented in the film *The Great Gatsby*.

■ **11** What errors of judgement can you find in Tom Buchanan's theory of society?

■ **12** At the end Nick Carraway and Jay Gatsby talk about their vision of the *American Dream*: Is there evidence in the film of a still continuing vision of realizing the eternal hope of a paradise on earth, the ideal democracy?

■ **13** Put your ideas together in the form of a diagram in which you illustrate the basic elements of The *American Dream*.

Myrtle and George Wilson

The second chapter of the film is dedicated to Tom's darling. Myrtle is introduced by a phone call disturbing Daisy's dinner party: *Tom has got a woman in New York.*

■ **1** How did Myrtle get acquainted with Tom?

■ **2** With reference to sequence [0:17:41–0:23:25] say why Tom is fascinated by Myrtle. Give also reasons for Myrtle's inclination towards Tom.

■ **3** Myrtle sums up her way of living in one phrase – which one?

Tom breaks Myrtle's nose after she has been continuously provoking him by calling Daisy.

■ **4** Consider the stills and describe how the film presents Tom and Myrtle's relationship.

■ **5** In reference to [0:22:59]: Analyse what Myrtle says about Tom.

■ **6** Write a description of Myrtle Wilson. Consider her relationship with Tom as well as her utterances about her husband George.

■ **7** Compare the two women, Daisy and Myrtle. What do they stand for in the context of the film?

★ *Maybe you think you can fool me ...* but you *can't fool God.* God sees *everything.*

★ *I'm not so dumb I don't know what's right from what's wrong.*

George's reply

George has found out about Myrtle's affair. They have a dispute about their relationship, in which Daisy accuses George of not having fulfilled her dreams.

Watch sequence [1:41:32–1:43:36].

■ **8** Evaluate what Myrtle says to George about their marriage.

Myrtle coldly mentions that what George is looking at is just an advertisement and that he is so dumb he doesn't know he's alive.

George seems to be lost and gets frantic about the events.

■ **9** What filmic means are used to show George's mental condition?

After the quarrel George leaves the garage. He is carrying a paper bag with a gun and the almighty Dr Eckleburg is looking down at him.

■ **10** After Myrtle's death George is confused and wants to take revenge on Tom, whom he regards as guilty because he knows about their affair. What does the still suggest?

Further studies:

■ **11** Comment on George's philosophy of *fixing it right.*

■ **12** Imagine you are George Wilson and your wife arrives home with a broken nose. Draw up a dialogue between the two. Keep in mind what you know about their relationship.

Tragic Irony in 'The Great Gatsby'

When Tom, Jordan and Nick call for petrol on their way to New York, George Wilson seems to be physically sick. Nick glances from Tom to George, he realizes that the two men have made the same discovery about their wives.

★ *I'm sick … I've been sick all day.*

1:33:33

1:34:34

■ **1** Evaluate the reactions of George and Tom.

■ **2** With regard to the affairs of Tom and Myrtle, Gatsby and Daisy: In what way is irony expressed in these stills? What is the specific tragic moment in these events?

INFO

Tragic irony is a device whereby ironic incongruity is introduced into the very structure of the plot, by having the spectators aware of elements in the situation of which one or more of the characters involved are ignorant. The words and actions thus have, in addition to their natural tragic impact and their value as furthering the action of the play, the peculiar relief which they derive from the contrast between the spectators' knowledge and the characters' ignorance.

Joseph T. Shipley, Dictionary of Literary Terms, Boston 1979, p. 169.

In tragic irony, the words and actions of the characters contradict the real situation, e.g. in Shakespeare's play Romeo and Juliet Romeo finds Juliet in a death-like sleep caused by drugs, but he assumes her to be dead and kills himself. When Juliet awakes and recognizes her dead lover she kills herself with his dagger.

Jordan tells Nick that she is engaged with another man and adds:

★ *Nevertheless you did throw me over …*
You said a bad driver was only safe until she met another bad driver? Well, I met another bad driver, didn't I? I mean it was careless of me to make such a wrong guess. I thought you were rather an honest, straightforward person.

The Great Gatsby, p. 154

Watch sequence [2:12:08–2:14:51].

■ **3** Comment on the use of tragic irony in the sequence.

The Valley of Ashes

The Valley of Ashes – the death of the 'American Dream'

One of the major themes in Fitzgerald's *The Great Gatsby* is the death of the *American Dream*. For the people in this novel the *American Dream* is the pursuit of life, liberty, and happiness.

So Gatsby's dream, the reason why he came to West Egg, is to reunite himself with his lost love, Daisy Fay. Gatsby desperately tried to liberate himself from poverty by acquiring millions of dollars and then he wanted to pursue a carefree life with Daisy. Unfortunately, the way Gatsby accumulated his wealth was through organized crime.

Fitzgerald shows that dreams achieved by illegal means can never be truly achieved:
Nick suggests: *All the immoral people have all the money.* This proverb refers to all the wealthy people he meets.

This mass of immorality and death converges on one distinct place, the Valley of Ashes, situated between West Egg and New York City:

This valley of ashes is a fantastic farm where ashes grow like wheat ridges and hills and grotesque gardens, where ashes take the forms of houses and chimneys and rising smoke and finally, with a transcendent effort, of men who move dimly and already crumbling through powdery air.

The Great Gatsby, p. 24

■ **1** With regard to the extract from Fitzgerald's novel and the still comment on the portrayal of the Valley of Ashes in the film.

0:40:52

1:44:10

1:53:13

■ **2** Look at the stills. Jot down your first reactions to the stills. Discuss your ideas in class.

★ *About half way between the two Eggs and New York the motor-road hastily joins the railroad and runs beside it for a short distance presided over by the eyes of Dr T. J. Eckleburg – set there by some wild way of an oculist, who set them there to fatten his practice in the borough of Queens.*

[0:13:44–0:14:03]

Wilson: What you're trying to do is not right, Myrtle. I'm a trusting kind of fellow. I don't think no harm to nobody. But when I know a thing, I know it. Maybe you think you can fool me, Myrtle. Maybe you can. But you can't fool God. God sees everything.

Myrtle: That's an advertisement!

[1:41:32–1:42:48]

Watch [0:13:44–0:14:03], [1:41.32–1:42:48].

■ **3** After watching the two sequences and reading the quotations from the film: What do you think is the function of Dr T. J. Eckleburg?

In the novel there are more references to the characteristics of Dr T. J. Eckleburg:

The eyes of Doctor T. J. Eckleburg are blue and gigantic – their retinas are one yard high. They look out of no face but, instead, from a pair of enormous yellow spectacles which pass over a nonexistent nose. ... But his eyes, dimmed a little by many paintless days under sun and rain, brood on over the solemn dumping ground ... . *p. 24, ll. 12–21*

I followed him ... under Doctor Eckleburg's persistent stare ... . *p. 25, ll. 38–40*

Over the ash heaps the giant eyes of Doctor T. J. Eckleburg kept their vigil ... . *p. 110 ll. 3–4*

Watch [0:13:44–0:16:16], [0:57:04–0:58:39], [1:31:10–1:34:34], [1:41:32–1:43:36], [1:48:48–1:52:26].

4 Now describe how the director manages to establish a symbolic meaning of the billboard with the help of filmic devices.
▸ Check *Selected terms for film analysis* for further information on film technique: www.cornelsen.de/abi-e

There are only a few shops in this area, some are for rent and others appear unprosperous and bare, being a part of this waste land. And then there is a garage – George B. Wilson's garage.

5 Look at Wilson's garage. What do you think the director wants to suggest to the viewer?

6 Looking at The Valley of Ashes as a setting and at George Wilson as a character, discuss: What does the film show about the the *American Dream*?

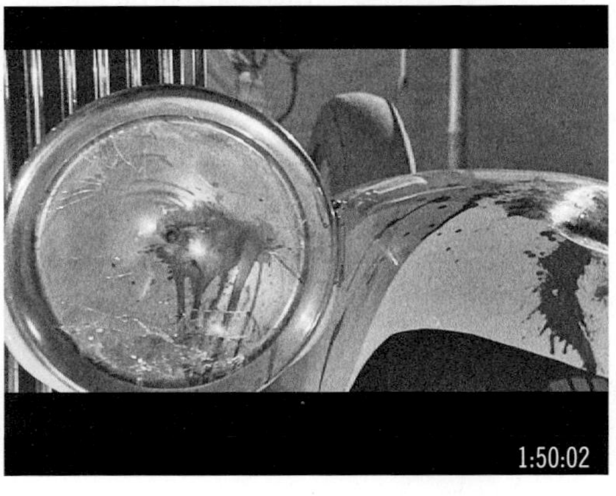

The eyes of God – or just the huge retinas of Dr Eckleburg?

■ **7** Compare the stills and describe what devices the film uses to convey the intended impression.

■ **8** What does God (i.e. Dr Eckleburg) see at this moment? How does the camera show the tragedy?

Nick Carraway – The narrator of the story

★ *In my younger and more vulnerable years my father gave me some advice that I've been turning over in my mind ever since. 'Whenever you feel like criticizing anyone,' he told me, 'just remember that all the people in this world haven't had the advantages that you've had.' In consequence I'm inclined to reserve all my judgements.*

[0:03:22–0:03:58]

Watch [0:03:22–0:05:41].

■ **1** Describe how the film introduces the narrator.

■ **2** Although Nick Carraway spends a lot of time with the Buchanans and Gatsby he remains an outsider. Describe how this is made clear with the help of filmic devices. Find other sequences that make his role as an outsider clear.

■ **3** It is through Nick's eyes and Nick's judgements that we learn about the events around Gatsby in the summer of 1922. Explain what makes Nick the perfect narrator of the story. In doing so take both his character and his relationship to the other characters into consideration. The film quotations from *Jay Gatsby – How is the character introduced?* (pp. 26) can help .

While Jordan is playing golf, Nick and Daisy are sitting on a bench talking:

Daisy: I'm going to arrange a marriage between you and Jordan. I'll sort of fling you together, lock you up accidentally in the linen closet or push you out to sea in a boat. All that sort of thing.
Nick: Daisy, I have no money. Would Jordan marry a man with no money?
Daisy: Of course not! Oh, well! It'll just have to be an affair, then.

[0:24:19–0:26:40]

Watch [0:57:04–0:57:58], [2:12:08–2:14:51].

■ **4** Although Nick is obviously attracted to Jordan, more than money seems to stand in the way of a marriage between them. Make a list of Jordan's character traits that either attract or repel Nick.

■ **5** [0:57:50]: Interpret the still. What do the film makers want to suggest?

Nick: You are a rotten driver!
Jordan: We missed it, didn't we?
Nick: You either ought to be more careful or you oughn't to drive at all.
Jordan: Let the other people be careful. It takes two to make an accident.
Nick: Suppose you meet somebody as careless as yourself.
Jordan: I hope I never will. I hate careless people. That's why I like you.

[0:57:04–0:57:58]

■ **6** With reference to Jordan's quotations explain why the relationship between the two of them broke up in the end.

■ **7** In sequence [2:12:08–2:14:51] it is made clear both by means of dialogue and filmic devices that Nick despises the affluent society of the East. Watch the sequence again and read the following dialogue. Explain how this is made clear to the viewer.

Nick:	She didn't send flowers, no message, nothing.
Jordan:	How could she?
Nick:	She could have done something, if she'd wanted. They're careless people, Tom and Daisy. They smash things up and then they retreat back into their money, or vast carelessness, or whatever it is that keeps them together, leaving other people to clean up the mess.
Jordan:	I had lunch with them today.
Nick:	Oh.
Jordan:	They're staying here. They're going to Europe for a few weeks while their new house is being prepared.
Nick:	I'm going away, too, only I'm going back West. I'm too squeamish and provincial for the East.
Jordan:	Is that why you threw me over? Something about … bad drivers?
Nick:	And taking two to make an accident.
Tom:	Nick, how are you? Nice to see you. …. Aren't you going to shake my hand? … What's the matter with him?
Nick:	What did you tell Wilson, Tom?
Tom:	Wilson? I told him the truth. If I hadn't told him who owned the car he would've killed me. Nick … Gatsby had it coming to him. He ran over Myrtle like you'd run over a dog and never even bothered to stop his car. Nick … I've had my share of suffering, too, you know. I went back to Myrtle's flat … and I looked at that little box of dog bisuits. And I sat down and cried like a baby.
Nick:	Tom … Don't you realize …

★ ....

....

Daisy:	Nick! Nick! How lovely to see you! …. I've been meaning to call you for days, but I've been so busy with the new house, you can't imagine. You have to promise to come and see us just as soon as we get back. You'll be our first guest. Promise.
Tom:	We've got to go, darling. Nick, Jordan. See you, Jordan.
Daisy:	You know how I love to see you at my table.
Nick:	Oh, Daisy.

★ ....

....

[0:57:04–0:57:58]

■ **8** Write an interior monologue for Nick in the thought bubbles.

Watch [1:40:01–1:40:34].

Just after Daisy has told Tom in the Plaza Hotel that she will leave him and has run away, Nick is very thougthful. Then he suddenly says:

★ *I just realized today is my birthday.*

■ **9** Explain the significance of this statement for Nick's character and his relationship towards the others.

Nick Carraway comes to the conclusion:

★ *... this has been a story of the West, after all – Tom and Gatsby, Daisy and Jordan and [he], were all Westerners, and perhaps [they] possessed some deficiency in common which made [them] subtly unadaptable to Eastern life.*

After watching the whole film ...

■ **10** Discuss this statement in the context of the film.

Film Review: The Great Gatsby

A Lavish 'Gatsby' Loses Book's Spirit: The Cast

The newest, biggest, most expensive and longest screen version of *The Great Gatsby*, which had its premiere here last night, moves spaniel-like through F. Scott Fitzgerald's text, sniffing and staring at events and objects very close up with wide, mopey eyes, seeing almost everything and comprehending practically nothing. The film begins its regular engagement at four theaters today.

The language is right, even the chunks of exposition that have sometimes been turned into dialogue. The sets and costumes and most of the performances are exceptionally good, but the movie itself is as lifeless as a body that's been too long at the bottom of a swimming pool.

Francis Ford Coppola, who wrote the screenplay, and Jack Clayton, the director, have treated the book as if it were an illustrated encyclopedia of the manners and morals of the nineteen-twenties instead of a short, elegiacal romantic novel whose idiosyncratic beat demands something more perceptive from the moviemakers than mere fidelity to plot.

The Great Gatsby has been filmed twice before, first with Warner Baxter and Lois Wilson in 1926, the year after it was published. It was done again in 1949 with Alan Ladd playing the title role, the elegant young roughneck, Jay Gatsby, a part-time bootlegger and swindler whose smile according to Fitzgerald, possessed the quality of 'eternal reassurance', and with Betty Field as Daisy Buchanan, the pretty, easily distracted rich girl who became for Gatsby all there was to hope for in the American Dream.

Though I didn't see the first version and remember very little of the second, I can't imagine that either could have been conceived with the care that went into this production. Why, then, should this *Gatsby* be so lugubrious, threatening at times to turn into the longest movie ever made?

The answer I suspect, is the all-too-reverential attitude. It completely mistakes the essence of Fitzgerald's novel, which is not in its story but in its headlong, elliptical literary style that dazzles us by the manner in which it evokes character and event, rather than with the characters and events themselves.

Nothing that Mr. Clayton does with the actors or with the camera comes close to catching the spirit of Fitzgerald's impatient brilliance. The film transforms *Gatsby* into a period love story that seems to take itself as solemnly as *Romeo and Juliet*. The plot has been dismantled like an

4 *mopey* sad
7 *chunk* a large piece or amount of something
14 *elegiacal* feeling sad about something
14 *idiosyncratic* unusual
27 *lugubrious* very sad or serious
29 *all-too-reverential* showing too much respect and admiration
31 *dazzle* prevent from seeing clearly because of bright light
37 *dismantle* take something apart so that it is in separate pieces

antique engine and photographed, piece by piece, preserved in lots of pretty, glistening images that bathe the film in nostalgia as thick as axle grease.

If reverence is one part of the problem, the other part is a stunning lack of cinematic imagination. The film's big set pieces – the wild parties at Gatsby's Long Island mansion – are almost embarrassingly awkward in their staging, the flappers and their beaux always caught doing their Charlestons at the same orgiastic pitch, like the figures on some complicated wind-up Bavarian toy.

Some of the movie's best moments are hardly more than recitations, as when the narrator, Nick Carraway (Sam Waterston), opens the film with a soundtrack exposition that sets the time, place and characters. This includes the marvelous line in which Nick tells us how Daisy and Tom Buchanan, before moving to Long Island that fatal summer, had 'drifted here and there unrestfully, wherever people played polo and were rich together.'

Although Robert Redford is hardly an ideal choice to play Gatsby – he looks so Ivy League it's difficult to believe that he didn't prep at Choate – he's a good enough actor to carry the role without damaging the film. [...]

Mia Farrow is lovely, eccentric and unfathomable as Daisy, which may be an impossible role, one that is much more easily accepted on the page than on the screen. I also liked Bruce Dern as her husband, a guy so securely rich and well-born he can be a slob, Mr. Waterston as Nick who, like Gatsby, remains an outsider in the society he inhabits, and Karen Black and Scott Wilson, as Myrtle and George Wilson, whose lives, like Gatsby's, are so casually destroyed by the Buchanans.

As Fitzgerald wrote it, *The Great Gatsby* is a good deal more than an ill-fated love story about the cruelties of the idle rich. Though set in Long Island, it is very much about the Middle West. All of its major characters have moved east, from Minnesota (Gatsby), from Chicago (Nick and Tom), from Louisville (Daisy), literally reversing the direction of the migrations that established the American civilization, thus marking its doom. The movie can't see this through all its giant close-ups of pretty knees and dancing feet. It's frivolous without being much fun.

By VINCENT CANBY Published: March 28, 1974 in: The New York Times

39–40 *axle grease* Achsenfett
44 *beau (old-fashioned)* a woman's close friend or lover
46 *wind-up Bavarian toy* a toy that has to be wound up in order to make it move or start working
55 *Ivy League* refers to a number of especially prestigious eastern US universities
55 *prep at Choate* have a scholarship at a prestigious boarding school
58 *unfathomable* too mysterious to be understood
61 *slob (informal)* someone who is lazy
72 *frivolous* not serious or sensible

■ **1** Summarize the author's opinion about the film.

■ **2** The author basically criticizes the film because it 'loses the book's spirit'.
Not having read the novel, do you agree that the film is 'frivolous without being much fun' and that it cannot make it clear that the American civilization is doomed (ll. 59ff.)?

■ **3** Analyse the language the author uses to make his point clear.

■ **4** Analyse the structure of the review: In which passages do you learn something about the plot, the actors, the director, etc. and in which passages does the author express his opinion about the film?

■ **5** Collect useful phrases for writing a review from the given text.

■ **6** Write your own review of *The Great Gatsby*.

Film evaluation sheet

As the film runs, answer the following questions using specific details from the film.

- How is the setting established in the film?
- How are the main characters introduced?
- How is the conflict introduced?
- Describe a sequence you thought was very convincing and explain why.
- Describe a sequence that could be improved. Outline how.
- What is the climax of the film? How do the filmmakers lead up to it?
- What do you take as the message of the film?
- Would you recommend this film to other cinema classes? Why/why not?
- Would you recommend this film to friends? Why/why not?

▸ **Your emotional response to the film:**

▸ **Purpose/aim of the film as you see it:**

Final verdict: ◯ very favourable ◯ favourable ◯ unfavourable ◯ uncertain

Photography:	shot, focus, frame, camera angle, camera movement, space, setting, lighting, colour
Sound:	music, dialogue, silence, language, synchronicity, sound effects
Editing:	order, transition, cuts, duration, rhythm, continuity, disjuncture, montage, motifs
Narration:	story/plot, dramatic appeal, motivation, logic, closure, point of view
Other:	self-reference, realism/representation, art, politics, values/ideology, historical context

- Describe what are for you the most striking features that characterize this film. Refer to the terms above: Circle the terms you'd like to use in your argument.